IRAQ: A WAR

IRAQ: A WAR

introduction by Chris Hedges

photographs by the Associated Press

OLIVE
BRANCH
PRESS

An imprint of Interlink Publishing Group, Inc.
www.interlinkbooks.com

First published in 2007 by

OLIVE BRANCH PRESS
An imprint of Interlink Publishing Group, Inc.
46 Crosby Street
Northampton, Massachusetts 01060
www.interlinkbooks.com

Published simultaneously in Germany by Melzer Verlag GmbH, Neu Isenburg

Interior design: V.Barl
Cover design: Juliana Spear

ISBN 1-56656-648-7
ISBN 13: 978-1-56656-648-3

Library of Congress Cataloging-in-Publication Data
Iraq : a war / introduction by Chris Hedges ; photographs by the Associated Press.—
1st American ed.
     p. cm.
 ISBN 1-56656-648-7 (pbk.)
1. Iraq War, 2003—Pictorial works. I. Hedges, Chris. II. Associated Press.
 DS79.762.I73 2006
 956.7044'3—dc22

                                                             2006012195

Printed and bound in China

To request our complete 40-page full-color catalog, please call us toll free at 1-800-238-LINK,
visit our website at www.interlinkbooks.com, or write to
Interlink Publishing, 46 Crosby Street, Northampton, MA 01060
e-mail: info@interlinkbooks.com

Introduction

by Chris Hedges

The vanquished know war. They see through the empty jingoism of those who use the abstract words of glory, honor, and patriotism to mask the cries of the wounded, the senseless killing, war profiteering, and chest-pounding grief. They know the lies the victors often do not acknowledge, the lies covered up in stately war memorials and mythic war narratives, filled with words of courage and comradeship. They know the lies that permeate the thick, self-important memoirs by amoral statesmen who make wars but do not know war.

The vanquished know the essence of war—death. They grasp that war is necrophilia. They see that war is a state of almost pure sin with its goals of hatred and destruction. They know how war fosters alienation, leads inevitably to nihilism, and is a turning away from the sanctity and preservation of life. All other narratives about war too easily fall prey to the allure and seductiveness of violence, as well as the attraction of the godlike power that comes with the license to kill with impunity.

But the words of the vanquished come later, sometimes long after the war, when grown men and women unpack the suffering they endured as children, what it was like to see their mother or father killed or taken away, or what it was like to lose their homes, their community, their security, and be discarded as human refuse. But by then few listen. The truth about war comes out, but usually too late. We are assured by the war-makers that these stories have no bearing on the glorious violent enterprise the nation is about to inaugurate. And, lapping up the myth of war and its sense of empowerment, we prefer not to look.

We see the war in Iraq primarily through the distorted lens of the occupiers. The embedded reporters and photographers, dependent on the military for food and transportation as well as security, have a natural and understandable tendency, one I have myself felt, to protect those who are protecting them. They are not allowed to report outside of the unit and are, in effect, captives. They have no relationships with the occupied, essential to all balanced reporting of conflicts, but only with the marines and soldiers who drive through desolate mud-walled towns and pump grenades and machine-gun bullets into houses, leaving scores of nameless dead and wounded in their wake. The reporters and photographers admire and laud these fighters for their physical courage. They feel protected as well by the jet fighters and heavy artillery and throaty rattle of machine guns. And the reporting, even among those who struggle to keep some distance, usually descends into a shameful cheerleading.

There is no more candor in Iraq or Afghanistan than there was in Vietnam, but in the age of live satellite feeds the military has perfected the appearance of candor. What we are fed is the myth of war. For the myth of war, the myth of glory and honor, sells newspapers and boosts ratings—real war reporting does not. Ask the grieving parents of Pat Tillman. Nearly every embedded war correspondent sees his or her mission as sustaining civilian and army morale. This is what passes for coverage. In wartime, as Senator Hiram Johnson reminded us in 1917, "truth is the first casualty."

All our knowledge of the war in Iraq has to be viewed as lacking the sweep and depth that will come one day, perhaps years from now, when a small Iraqi boy or girl reaches adulthood and unfolds for us the sad and tragic story of the invasion and bloody occupation of their nation.

For now, we see the reality of war in glimpses, snapshots, momentary truths, that allow us to peer briefly into the soulless endeavor undertaken in Iraq in our name. The photographs in this book must suffice. They capture in framed outlines the crushed and mangled remains of human beings, consumed in the maw of war, the godlike power of uniformed killers, who can murder and maim with impunity and who thrill darkly in the power to revoke another person's charter to live on this earth. They capture the desperation and grief of mothers as they clutch the remains of their dead children and the rows of newly dug graves, for war, at its essence, is about industrial slaughter, about death. You can see but not smell the awful effluvium of bloated corpses. You can see the combat high but not feel the fear. You can see the crushing of human life and hope, but not feel the heart being rent from the chest. All pictorial images of war are shadows, brief moments of intense human excitement and pain and desperation, frozen for us by a lens and the steady hand of a man or woman who does smell and taste the bitter intoxication of battle and death. The best of these photographs, and there are many, telegraph to us these raw emotions. These photographs stand, finally, as a monument to the courage of those who took them and expose the cold and cynical lies told to us to wage war. All are betrayed in war. This is the subtext of all these photographs. It is why they work. It is why they are honest.

I have spent most of my adult life in war. I began two decades ago covering wars in Central America, where I spent five years, then the Middle East, where I spent seven, and the Balkans where I covered the wars in Bosnia and Kosovo. My life has been marred, let me say deformed, by the organized industrial violence that year after year was an intimate part of my existence. I have watched young men bleed to death on lonely Central American dirt roads and cobblestone squares in Sarajevo. I have looked into the eyes of mothers, kneeling over the lifeless and mutilated bodies of their children. I have stood in warehouses with rows of corpses, including children, and breathed death into my lungs. I carry within me the ghosts of those I worked with, my comrades, now gone.

I have felt the attraction of violence. I know its seductiveness, excitement, and the powerful addictive narcotic it can become. The young soldiers, trained well enough to be disciplined but encouraged to maintain their naïve adolescent belief in invulnerability, have in wartime more power at their fingertips than they will ever have again. They catapult from being minimum-wage employees at places like Burger King, facing a life of dead-end jobs with little hope of health insurance and adequate benefits, to being part of, in the words of the marines, "the greatest fighting force on the face of the earth." The disparity between what they were and what they have become is breathtaking and intoxicating. This intoxication is only heightened in wartime when all taboos are broken. Murder goes unpunished and often rewarded. The thrill of destruction fills their days with wild adrenaline highs, strange grotesque landscapes that are hallucinogenic, all accompanied by a sense of purpose and comradeship. The experience of war overpowers the alienation many left behind. They become accustomed to killing, carrying out acts of slaughter with no more forethought than they take to relieve themselves. And the abuses committed against the helpless prisoners in Abu Ghraib or Guantanamo are not aberrations, but the true face of war. In wartime all human beings become objects, objects either to gratify or destroy or both. And almost no one is immune. The contagion of the crowd sees to that.

"Force," Simone Weil wrote, "is as pitiless to the man who possess it, or thinks he does, as it is to his victim. The second it crushes; the first it intoxicates."

As the war grinds forward, as we sink into a morass of our own creation, as our press and political opposition, and yes, even our great research universities, remain complacent and passive, as we refuse to confront the forces that have crippled us outside our gates and are working to cripple us within, the tyranny we impose on others begins to be imposed on us. In war, we always deform ourselves, our essence. We give up individual conscience—maybe even consciousness—for contagion of the crowd, the rush of patriotism, the belief that we must stand together as a nation in moments of extremity. To make a moral choice, to defy war's enticement, to find moral courage, can be self-destructive.

The attacks on the World Trade Center illustrate that those who oppose us, rather than coming from another moral universe, have been schooled well in modern warfare. The dramatic explosions, the fireballs, the victims plummeting to their deaths, the collapse of the towers in Manhattan, were straight out of Hollywood. Where else, but from the industrialized world, did the suicide bombers learn that huge explosions and death above a city skyline are a peculiar and effective form of communication? They have mastered the language we have taught them. They understand that the use of indiscriminate violence against innocents is a way to make a statement. We leave the same calling cards. We delivered such incendiary messages in Vietnam, Serbia, Afghanistan, and Iraq. It was Secretary of Defense Robert McNamara who in the summer of 1965 defined the bombing raids that would kill hundreds of thousands of civilians north of Saigon as a means of communication to the Communist regime in Hanoi.

The most powerful anti-war testaments, of war and what war does to us, are those that eschew images of combat. It is the suffering of the veteran whose body and mind are changed forever, the suffering and death of families and children caught up in the unforgiving crucible of war, which alone begin to tell the story of war. The wounds that forever mark a life, the wounds that leave faces and bodies horribly disfigured by burns or shrapnel, are the real marks of war. Those who do not show us the agony of the dying, who make war palatable and sanitized, are culpable for the slaughter. Those who permit us to taste war's perverse thrill, but who spare us from seeing war's consequences, only disseminate the plague of war. The wounded and the dead, in these scenarios, are swiftly carted offstage. And for this lie I blame most of the press, which willingly hides from us the effects of bullets, roadside bombs, and rocket-propelled grenades. The press sat at the feet of those who lie to make this war possible and dutifully reported these lies and call it journalism. These photographs do not pander to this myth, this lie. They seek to tell the truth. They do not partake of this awful betrayal.

War is, finally, always about betrayal. It is about the betrayal of the young by the old, idealists by cynics and finally soldiers by politicians. Those who pay the price, those who are maimed forever by war are crumpled up and thrown away. We do not see them. We do not hear them. They are doomed, like wandering spirits, to float around the edges of our consciousness, ignored, even reviled. The message they bring is too painful for us to hear. We prefer the abstractions of glory, honor, patriotism and heroism, the big thumping bands that play patriotic music and the tough words that pump us up as powerful and great. All these words and posturing, of course, in the terror and brutality of combat are empty, meaningless, and obscene. But those who sell us this myth do not know war. They will never know war.

We are losing the war in Iraq. We are an isolated and reviled nation. We are pitiless to others weaker than ourselves. We have lost sight of our democratic ideals. This is the truth about Iraq; it is truth these photographs work to convey. Thucydides wrote of Athens expanding empire and how this empire led it to become a tyrant abroad and then a tyrant at home. The tyranny Athens imposed on others it finally imposed on itself. If we do not confront the lies and hubris told to justify the killing and mask the destruction carried out in our name in Iraq, if we do not grasp the moral corrosiveness of empire and occupation, if we continue to allow force and violence to be our primary form of communication, if we do not remove from power our flag-waving, cross-bearing versions of the Taliban, we will not so much defeat dictators such as Saddam Hussein as become them.

British Royal Marines occupy the oil fields on the al-Faw peninsula.
Terry Richards

pages 10 & 11
March 19, 2003: US infantry combat vehicles on their way to the Iraqi border. A day earlier, President Bush had issued an ultimatum to Iraqi President Saddam Hussein to leave the country within 48 hours.
Jean-Marc Bouju

pages 12 & 13
Soldiers from the 101st Airborne in the Kuwaiti desert before their decampment. More than 300,000 soldiers of the coalition troops had positioned their forces in the Middle East. *John Moore*

A wire-controlled rocket hits an Iraqi armored tank. *John Moore*

A dead Iraqi soldier under his vehicle, near Mosul.
Kamal Osman

Iraqi soldiers escape along the bank of the Tigris. American armored vehicles encountered ineffectual resistance and advanced into the center of Baghdad. *Jerome Delay*

Refinery workers try to extinguish the fire set by militants at Iraq's biggest refinery in al-Fath. *Bassem Daham*

pages 18 & 19
In the foreground, a car-ferry crosses the Tigris 10 km (6.2 miles) south of Kirkuk. Behind, an oil pipeline goes up in flames. *Bassem Daham*

The oil pipeline to the Turkish harbor Ceyhan is in
flames. Protecting the oil transporting system across the
Iraqi desert is almost impossible. *Bassem Daham*

pages 22 & 23
A British marine on the al-Faw peninsula fires
a Milan anti-tank missile at an Iraqi position.
Jon Mills

Above: American Marines blow up and attack a house entrance in
Ramadi. *Jim MacMillan*

Right: Marine soldiers give their comrades covering fire during the
storming of an Iraqi military headquarters. *Laura Rauch*

Above: A 10-meter-high statue of Saddam Hussein is blasted from its plinth in Tikrit. *Saurabh Das*

Right: In Tikrit, American soldiers make a basketball court out of the enormous entry hall of one of Saddam's palaces. *Efrem Lukatsky*

Under police supervision, young people carry furniture from a destroyed house in Hilla, south of Baghdad. *Brennan Linsley*

Looting in Basra. *Anja Niedringhaus*

A US soldier naps in one of Saddam's palaces in Tikrit,
the political stronghold of the Ba'ath regime.
Gregorio Borgia

Inside a Bradley armored vehicle before deployment to Samara, an hour north of Baghdad. *Stefan Zaklin*

A US soldier sits on packs of Iraqi dinars that were removed from a bank. *Hussein Malla*

An Iraqi woman screams when her wounded husband and son are turned away from the overcrowded al-Kindi hospital in Baghdad. *Jerome Delay*

On May 1, 2003, with a large "Mission Accomplished" banner behind him on the *USS Abraham Lincoln*, President Bush declares to the nation that the "battle for Iraq" is won and the major combat operations are finished. At that point, 171 coalition troops had died in the war. Since that speech, another 2,341 coalition troops have died. And according to Iraq Body Count, at least 33,638 civilians have died—a number feared to be low because of the difficulty of collecting such information.
J. Scott Applewhite

An Iraqi and his son watch President Bush's May 2004 apology and contention that abuse at Abu Ghraib was confined to a few people. *Muhammed Muheisen*

A soldier in a Stryker armored vehicle in Mosul. The Stryker, the army's newest armored vehicle, has been criticized for being too lightly protected for the dangers of warfare in Iraq.
Jim MacMillan

US Marines pose after battles in Falluja for a press
photo. *Anja Niedringhaus*

The giant statue of Saddam Hussein in front of the presidential palace in Baghdad, toppled. Pictures of the fallen statue were shown widely in the US media as evidence of the overthrow of the man himself.
Anja Niedringhaus

Right: Iraqi men fight for the humanitarian aid being delivered by the Kuwaiti Red Crescent in Safwan, in southern Iraq. *Anja Niedringhaus*

The Italian bishop Angelo Bagnasco during a mass with Italian soldiers in Nasiriya. *Laurent Rebours*

pages 38 & 39
Iraqis at a Friday prayer in Sadr City, before leaving for a demonstration against the occupation. *Karim Kadim*

A British bishop holds a service at a military cemetery near al-Kut.
Hundreds of British and colonial Indian soldiers were buried hereo after
they were defeated by the Ottomans in World War I.
Brennan Linsley

pages 42 & 43
The Ashura festival commemorates the death of Hussain, the Third Shi'a
Imam and grandson of the Prophet. Here at the Imam Hussain Mosque
in Karbala in 2004, more than a million believers come together for the
festival, demonstrating the new political power of Shiites in Iraq. (During
the Ba'ath regime, huge processions were banned.) *Brennan Linsley*

Shiite cleric Muqtada al-Sadr speaks in front of his house in Najaf. *Mohammed Hato*

pages 44 & 45
Shiites sway the Iraqi flag from Saddam's era and hold up a picture of Muqtada al-Sadr. In June 2003, al-Sadr formed the al-Mahdi army, opposing the US occupation. *Hadi Mizban*

A photo gallery of Shiite martyrs. This exhibition was organized by the Islamic Dawa party, of which former Prime Minister Ibrahim al-Jafari is a member. *Samir Mizban*

A wall painting in Sadr City that shows scenes from the history of Shia Islam. Sixty percent of the Iraqis are Shiites. Together with the Kurds they control the National Assembly and the government. *Karim Kadim*

A Mandean, or Sabean, reading his holy scriptures during the New Year celebration. About 150,000 Sabeans live in Iraq, practicing a faith whose scriptures draw on ancient Babylonian, Zoroastrian, and Manichean beliefs. Since the occupation, Sabeans and Christians alike have occasionally been the targets of fundamentalist riots. *Karim Kadim*

A Shiite woman from Karbala cooks rice for the pilgrims during the Ashura festival. *Hussein Malla*

Religion, as practiced at war in the Mesopotamian desert. *Tony Nicoletti*

pages 50 & 51
Another kind of prayer. *Laura Rauch*

A US armored vehicle at a checkpoint in Falluja. US troops attacked the town with almost 15,000 ground troops, twice. *Anja Niedringhaus*

Soldiers in the rubble of the Canal Hotel, the former UN headquarters in Baghdad. The complex was destroyed by a missile attack in August 2003. Twenty people, among them Sergio Vieira de Mello, the high commissioner for human rights, were killed. One hundred people were injured. *Sergie Grits*

An empty street in the city of Falluja, where more than
200,000 citizens once lived. Although the Americans
made it nearly impossible for the press to cover the April
2004 siege, eyewitnesses have reported the death of at
least 600 civilians—many of them women and children.
Anja Niedringhaus

US soldiers looking for insurgents, who were thought to control many police stations in Mosul. *Jim MacMillan*

US Marines on their way to downtown Falluja. The city fell after days of bloody battles in the houses and streets. *Jim MacMillan*

A US Marine carries a GI Joe mascot for luck in Falluja. The military said that 31 Americans were killed in the siege. *Anja Niedringhaus*

Falluja was mainly defended by young Sunnis. Based on official information, 1,200 to 1,500 Iraqi fighters were killed during the siege of the city. *Jim MacMillan*

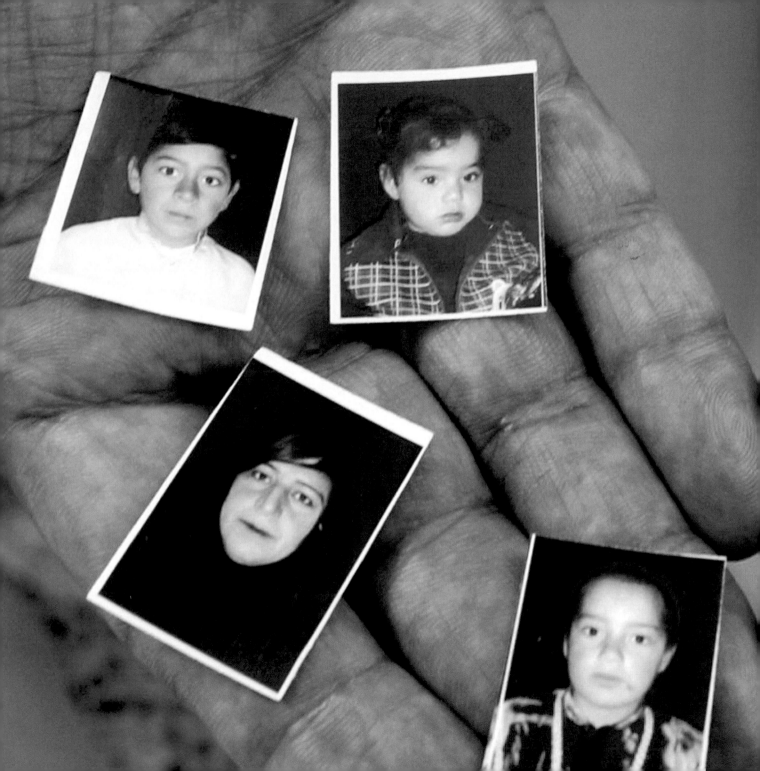

Mohammed Saleem, 18 months, lies in a coffin in a Sadr City morgue. He was killed, along with four other family members, when US forces opened fire on their car.
Karim Kadim

pages 58 & 59
An Iraqi shows pictures of his family; they were killed when a US helicopter fired on wedding festivities in Ramadi.
Anja Niedringhaus

The mother of Samah Hussein grieves over her son. The boy
was among twelve people reportedly killed by a suicide car
bombing outside a US military camp.
Samir Mizban

pages 62 & 63
Iraqis at the graves of relatives and friends killed in the siege of
Falluja. A former soccer field had to be turned into a cemetery
to accommodate the victims. *Muhammed Muheisen*

pages 64 & 65
American observation posts at the Syrian border.
Bassem Tellawi

An Iraqi policeman shows a mortar shell found along with other ammunition and various arms during a house inspection in the south of Baghdad. *Hadi Mizban*

Right: Nearly three years after the war began, 130,000 US soldiers are stationed in Iraq. *Brennan Linsley*

Children from Falluja watch US soldiers at a checkpoint.
Families were allowed to return to their destroyed city when the
battles were over. *John Moore*

pages 68 & 69
Patrol in Samara. *Jim MacMillan*

An Iraqi woman and a US soldier talking in a school in
Baghdad. *Mohammed Uraibi*

A member of the newly founded national guard on patrol in Sadr City. Many guards wear face masks so they cannot be identified by the rebels of al-Sadr's Mahdi army. *John Moore*

Left: Women carry water near Basra, in southern Iraq. *Dan Chung*

A student in a Kirkuk elementary school holds a picture of President Bush. Some Kurds, as well as Shiites, believed that the invasion would improve their lot. *Kevin Frayer*

A British soldier with his German shepherd on a patrol
near the southern Iraqi harbor town Umm Qasr. In this
area, criminal activities increased after the invasion.
David Cheskin

Iraqi policemen hold a picture of al-Sadr at a demonstration.
A considerable contingent of the police force was recruited from
supporters of the Shiite parties. *Karim Kadim*

A US soldier guards the main entrance of the train station in Kirkuk, where conflict simmered between Kurds and Arabs even before the invasion forces arrived. *Sasa Kralj*

A private security guard in front of the French embassy in Baghdad. More than 20,000 security guards from all over the world work in Iraq. While the pay is good (US$ 700 a day), the risk is great: by the middle of 2005, more than 200 had been killed. *Hussein Malla*

A rebel in Najaf has a picture of Muqtada al-Sadr on his anti-tank missile launcher. Al-Sadr, who comes from a long line of clerics, is a vociferous opponent of the US occupation and proponent of an Islamist central government. *Hadi Mizban*

A devoted Shiite flagellates himself during a ritual commemorating the death in 680 of Hussein, grandson of the Prophet Mohammad. Hussein is venerated as a martyr. *Hadi Mizban*

A member of a militant group barricades himself in a house in Baquba after attacking a US convoy. *Mohammad Adnan*

pages 80 & 81
Rebels meet in Mosul, after attacking two US vehicle platoons. *AP stringer 4HJTJ*

An insurgent displays a remote-controlled drone shot down in Falluja. On the banner: "There is no God but God and Mohammad is his messenger." *Bilal Hussein*

Followers of Shiite cleric Muqtada al-Sadr during a break in the battles against US and Iraqi security forces in Najaf, which lasted for days. On the headband: "Support me, Mahdi." *Hadi Mizban*

Iraqi fighters. *Mohammed Uraibi*

Left: A man prays over his Qur'an. *John Moore*

An Iraqi man celebrates atop a burning US Humvee after an explosion that destroyed a building and set four Humvees on fire, killing at least one US soldier, on April 26, 2004. *Muhammad Muheisen*

Right: British soldiers hit by a Molotov cocktail at a demonstration by the jobless in Basra. *Nabil al-Jurani*

Triumph over burning US vehicles in Mosul...
AP stringer 4HJTG

... and in al-Dora, a suburb of Baghdad.
Jerome Delay

pages 90 & 91
Moments after a series of bomb blasts on the Muslim holiday of Ashura, an Iraqi youth runs past victims and debris in the holy city of Karbala. *Brennan Lisley*

pages 92 & 93
271 people were killed and 393 injured in a series of attacks in Karbala on March 2, 2004. *Brennan Lisley*

Victims of the Karbala bomb blasts on market carts.
Brennan Lisley

Iraqis rescue a man from the ruins of a building after a car bombing in central Baghdad on June 14, 2004. At least ten people were killed, including three foreigners who were rebuilding Iraqi power plants. *Mohammed Uraibi*

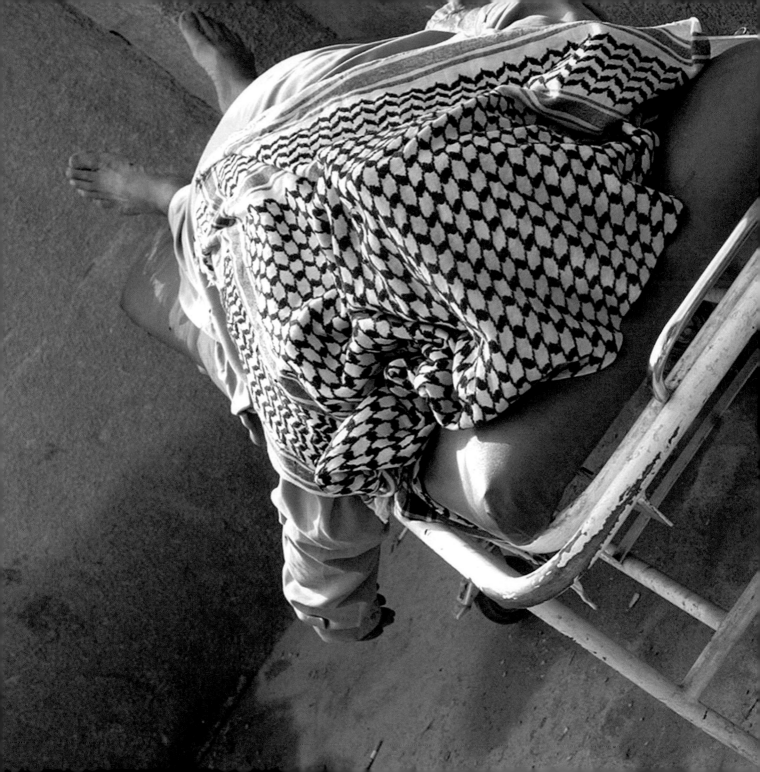

Abu Ghraib detainees before their release in June 2004. Most of them were imprisoned without charge. *Hussein Malla*

page 96 & 97
The victim of a bomb blast in Baghdad lies in the Yarmouk hospital morgue. *Jerome Delay*

A detained Iraqi man comforting his four-year-old son at a holding center for prisoners of war near Najaf, March 31, 2003. Putting hoods on detainees violates the Geneva Conventions. *Jean-Marc Bouju*

The hand of one of Saddam's victims, murdered in Abu Ghraib fourteen days after the beginning of the war. *Brennan Lisley*

An Abu Ghraib detainee waits for an official delegation in May 2004. *John Moore*

The US lost the goodwill of the victims of the Saddam regime when the Abu Ghraib abuse and torture scandal came to light. *Karim Kadim*

Female prisoners in Abu Ghraib have to undergo a strip search; for devoted Muslims this is particularly degrading. *John Moore*

The same holds true in the high-security building of the
disreputable prison. *John Moore*

A detainee in a solitary confinement cage talks with a
military policeman at Abu Ghraib. US soldiers said the
prisoner had frequently fought with other inmates.
June 22, 2004. *John Moore*

Maj. Geoffrey Miller, commander of US-run prisons in Iraq, apologizes
for "illegal and unauthorized operations" by a few soldiers in
Abu Ghraib. He was sent from Guantanamo to Iraq to introduce
Guantanamo's interrogation techniques. *John Moore*

Right: The little yellow-and-black phone, which works only in one
direction, is all the recourse available for the hundreds of relatives
and friends who go to the prison to request information.
Anja Niedringhaus

The image of Abu Ghraib they wanted the world to see. *John Moore*

Right: The sun sets on Abu Ghraib. *John Moore*

A provisional morgue in Haditha, northwest of Baghdad. All of the morgues in Iraq's bigger cities are overflowing.
Bilal Hussein

Women try to identify the remains of their relatives found in a mass grave in Mahaweel. More than 3,000 opponents of Saddam Hussein's regime who were killed after the Shiite revolt were buried here. *Alexander Zemlianichenko*

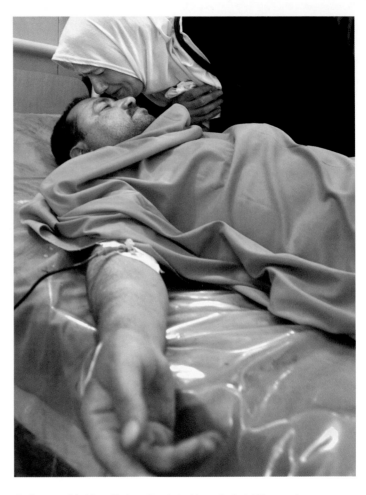

A wounded man with his wife in a Baghdad hospital. A US patrol shot at his car without apparent reason. *Hadi Mizban*

Iraqi men break down upon hearing of the death of one
of their colleagues, who was killed in a bomb blast in
Basra. *Nabil al-Jurani*

Iraqi national guardsmen with corpses of 48 comrades who
were ambushed and killed on their way home to their families.
AP stringer 4H1XB

In Baghdad, members of the Iraqi civil defense, set up by the US. In addition to the bomb attacks and political murders, criminal offenses have also spun out of control. *Brennan Lisley*

Murder in the middle of the day and on the open street...

… and an execution in front of a running camera.
AP stringer 41MA3, APTN

The effect of a mortar shell. *Khalid Mohammed*

An Arab Iraqi who was shot in the face in front of a polling station in Mosul. *Jim MacMillan*

Right: One of the several foreign truck drivers who were threatened with death on a daily basis if their Kuwaiti employers continued transporting for the occupiers. This was shown on television. *APTN (4DBZ7)*

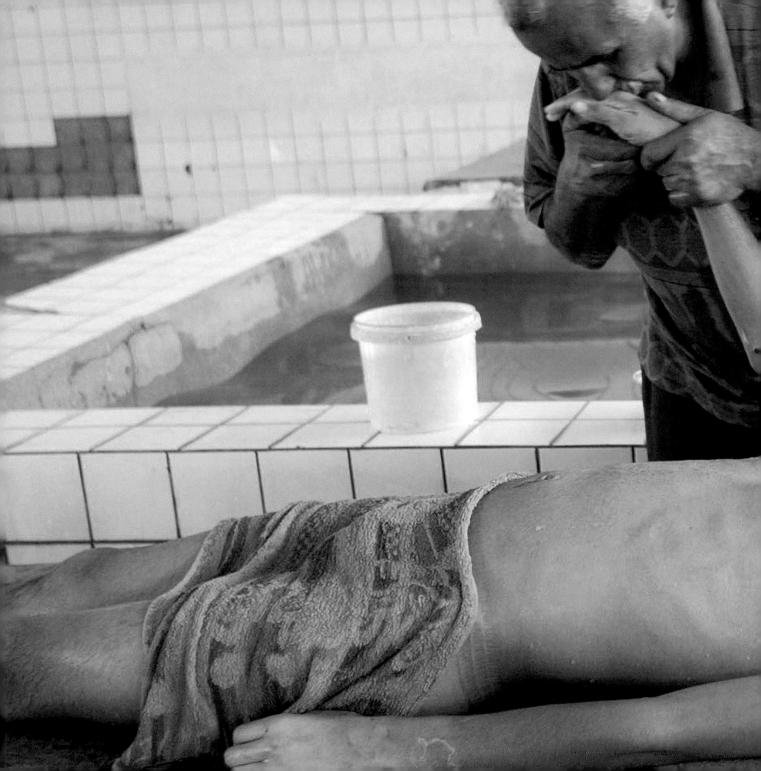

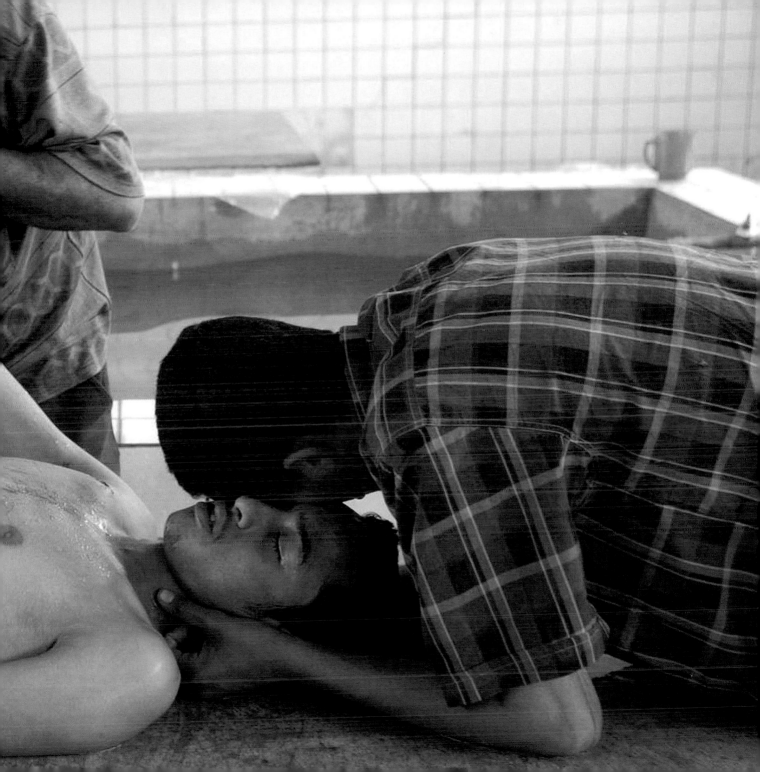

Mourning the victims of a car bomb attack in front of the oil ministry. *Hadi Mizban*

page 118 & 119
Ali Ahmed, age 16, was caught in crossfire in the holy city Najaf. His father and brother wash his corpse. *David Guttenfelder*

Right: Lunch under the picture of the Grand Ayatollah Ali al-Sistani, a religious leader of the Shiites. *Karim Kadim*

Shiites demonstrate in front of the Jordanian embassy after the Karbala attacks. *Khalid Mohammed*

pages 122 & 123
Polish soldiers in front of the reproduction of the fabled Babylonian Gate of Ishtar. *Pier Paolo Cito*

pages 124 & 125
During the festival of Ashura, devoted Shiites do penance for all those who did not come to help Hussein in the famous battle at Karbala. *Hussein Malla*

A demonstration against terrorism by electrical workers in Baghdad. After decades of control by the socialist Ba'ath party, secular ideas are more widespread in Iraq than in most countries of the Middle East. *Karim Kadim*

Shiite students take part in the Ashura rituals. Carrying swords copied from the 680 CE originals gives children the idea of defending their religion from a young age. The Mahdi army is shaped by these kinds of rituals. *Hussein Malla*

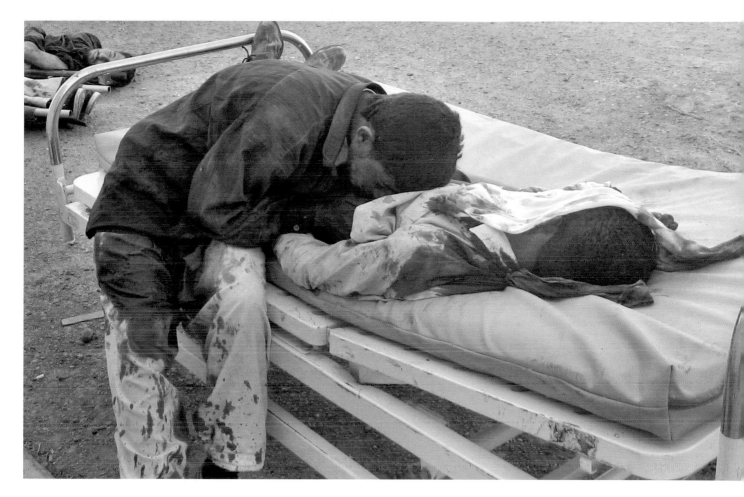

Jamil Abdul Husain grieves for his brother, Haydar Abdul Husain, 25, who was killed when a suicide car bomb exploded in a small market in Tikrit on May 11, 2005. At least 27 people were killed and 75 wounded. *Bassem Daham*

A dove sits on the shoulder of a Mahdi army soldier standing guard outside the ancient Imam Ali Mosque in Najaf. *Khalid Mohammed*

Right: Six-year-old Walid Samir does homework in a classroom in the al-Khadr school in Baghdad. *Muhammed Muheisen*

In a war in which the Geneva Conventions are not respected, it is perhaps no surprise that the Red Cross headquarters in Baghdad was demolished. *Anja Niedringhaus*

The Red Crescent, the Islamic equivalent of the Red
Cross, fared not much better. *Brennan Linsley*

The US ambassador and administrator of the occupation government, Paul Bremer, leaves Baghdad on June 28, 2004, after handing the government over to interim leader Iyad Allawi. *Staff Sgt. D. Myles Cullen*

Muqtada al-Sadr recommended painting a US flag on the ground in front of a mosque, so believers could walk over it. *Alaa al-Marjani*

pages 134 & 135
US soldiers inspect a "donkey rocket launcher" in Baghdad. Similar contraptions had been used to attack the oil ministry and two hotels. *Khalid Mohammed*

A wedding in Baghdad in May 2005. After years of terror
and war Iraqis try get back to a normal life.
Hadi Mizban

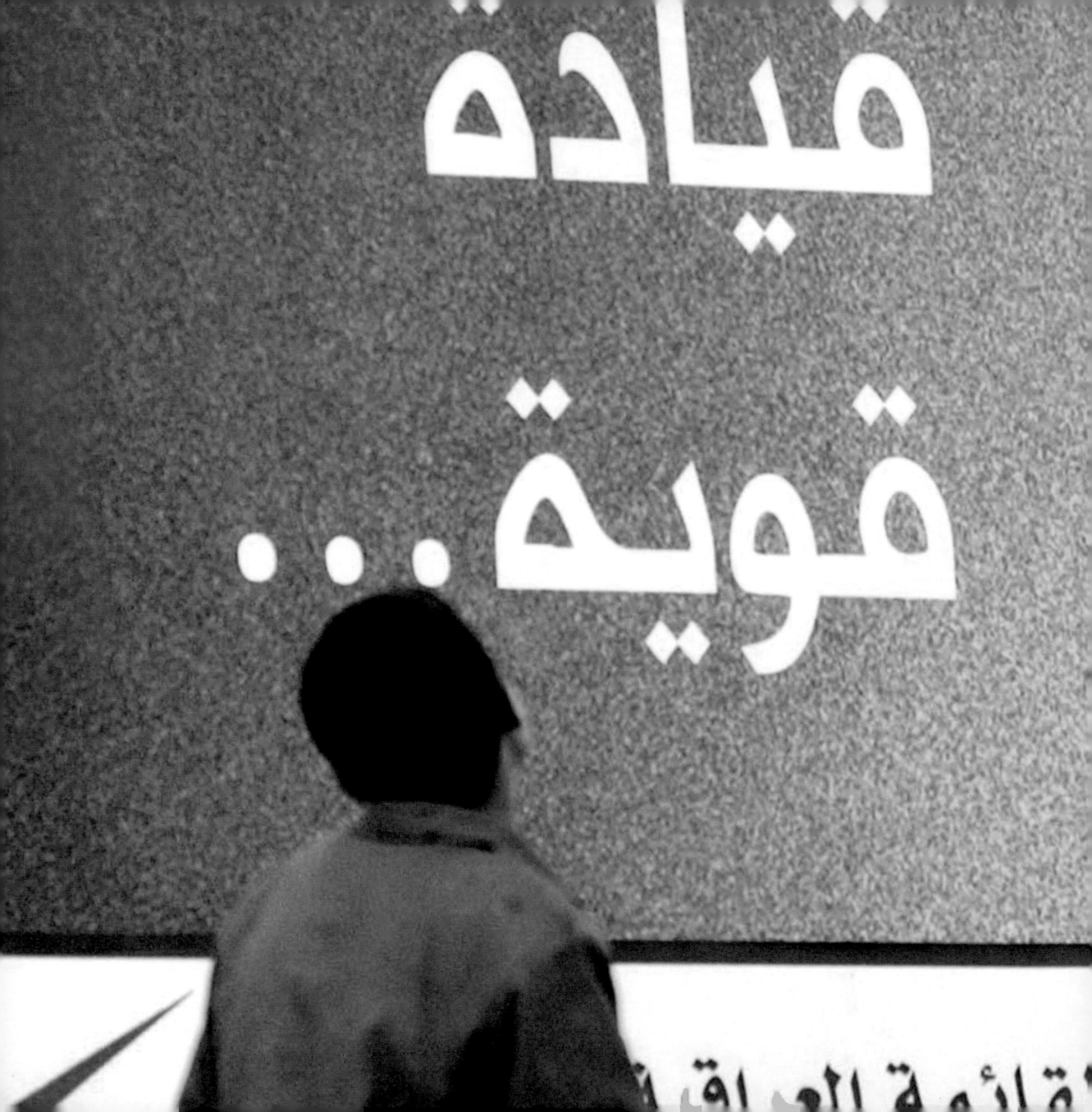
قيادة
قوية...

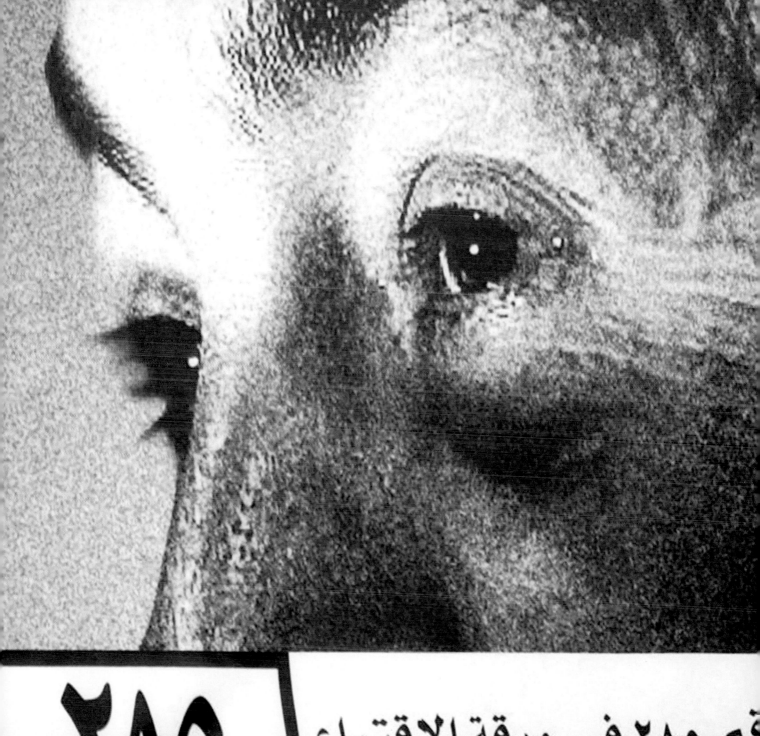

٢٨٥

قم ٢٨٥ فى ورقة الاقتراع

Old Iraqi dinars featuring Saddam Hussein's portrait
were replaced by new ones in October 2003.
Ivan Sekretarev

pages 138 & 139
Election poster of the US-promoted Iyad Allawi in Basra.
Richard Mills

Brokers at the Baghdad stock market. By the middle of 2004, 27 companies were listed. *Saeed Khan*

pages 142 & 143
On January 30, 2005, Iraqis line up to vote in southern Iraq. *Andrew Parsons*

pages 144 & 145
A son helps his father vote. *Andrew Parsons*

An unemployed former officer of the Iraqi air force thinks carefully before voting. *John Moore*

Left: An Iraqi man shows his purple ink-stained finger as proof of his voting. *John Moore*

Representatives of various tribes meet in Baghdad to discuss the new Iraqi constitution. *Khalid Mohammed*

A mixed group of politicians and representatives of tribes meet after the election at the Alwiya Club in Baghdad in February 2005. *Samir Mizban*

A picture of assemblywoman Lamia Abed Khadouri al-Sakri, who was the victim of an attack by Iraqis opposed to the US occupation.
Samir Mizban

A lonely assemblywoman at the new Iraqi National Assembly.
The diverse interests of Shiites, Sunnis, and Kurds made it
difficult to write one constitution. *Walthiq Khuzaie*

pages 152 & 153
The newly elected President Ibrahim al-Jafari (on the right) and
one of the four vice presidents, Ahmad Chalabi, under an image
of the Grand Ayatollah Ali al-Sistani. *Hadi Mizban*

A bride during a Shiite mass wedding in Najaf.
Alaa al-Marjani

The Photographers

Mohammed Adnan is a member of the Iraqi AP staff.

J. Scott Applewhite is the winner of two Pulitzer Prizes: in 1993 for pictures from the 1992 US presidential campaign and in 1999 for a series of pictures of the events surrounding President Clinton's impeachment.

Gregorio Borgia began working with the AP in Rome, worked as a stringer, and became a full staff member in 2005. His work includes three assignments in Iraq.

Jean-Marc Bouju was named World Press Photographer of the Year in 2003 for a color image that shows a detained Iraqi man comforting his four-year-old son at a holding center for prisoners of war near Najaf.

David Cheskin, of the AP and the Press Association, is a top British photographer who covers daily news in the UK. He won the Picture Editors' 2002 Getty Images Portfolio Award.

Dan Chung is one of the two Guardian staff members who cover the war in Iraq. He was the Nikon Press Photographer of the Year 2002 as well as the Guardian's 2004 Photographer of the Year.

Pier Paolo Cito was born in Italy and worked originally as a geologist. He joined the AP in 1998, and has covered conflict in Kosovo, Ethiopia, Israel–Palestine, as well as in Iraq.

Jerome Delay is an AP photographer who works in Baghdad. His globally awarded work has been published in *Time, Newsweek, Paris Match*, and *Stern*, as well as in daily newspapers around the world.

Kevin Frayer is a photojournalist who is married to the CTV's Middle East correspondent Janis Mackey Frayer.

Sergie Grits won the New York Society of Professional Journalists Deadline Club Best Feature Photo award for his picture of Afghani refugees.

David Guttenfelder has worked as a photographer for the AP in Kenya, Ivory Coast, Japan, and India. He was recently honored with the 2005 World Press Photo Prize in the category Daily Life, as well as the 2005 Photo of the Year by Editors & Publishers in both the Features and Photo Essay categories.

Bilal Hussein, a member of the Iraqi AP staff, remained in his hometown in order to document the battle for Falluja. He was part of the team that won the 2005 Pulitzer Prize in Breaking News Photography for depicting the bloody combat inside Iraqi cities.

Nabil al-Jurani is a freelance photographer who works for the AP in Iraq.

Karim Kadim is a member of the AP staff that won the 2005 Pulitzer Prize in the category Breaking News Photography.

Saeed Khan is a freelance photographer who specializes in digital photo enhancement and photo manipulation.

Wathiq Khuzaie has photographed extensively in Iraq; his images are frequently used by the AP and Getty Images.

Sasa Kralj is a Croatian photographer who was awarded a gold plaque at the Museum of Arts and Crafts Awards.

Brennan Linsley is a member of the AP staff that won the 2005 Pulitzer Prize in the category Breaking News Photography.

Efrem Lukatsky is an AP photographer who also covers daily news in the Ukraine and Uzbekistan.

Jim MacMillan is a *Philadelphia Daily News* photographer who was on the AP staff that won the 2005 Pulitzer Prize in the category Breaking News Photography.

Hussein Malla is an AP photographer from Lebanon, presently based in Beirut. He has worked extensively in the Middle East and also covered the US war in Afghanistan.

Jon Mills, a freelance photographer, was one of the 150 UK media correspondents who were invited to accompany British troops to Iraq. His award-winning pictures have been published in UK national papers, *Paris Match*, and *USA Today*.

Richard Mills is a photographer for the *Times* of London.

Hadi Mizban is a member of the Iraqi AP staff.

Samir Mizban, a member of the Iraqi AP staff, was part of the team that won the 2005 Pulitzer Prize in the category Breaking News Photography.

Khalid Mohammed, a member of the Iraqi AP staff in Baghdad, was part of the team that won the 2005 Pulitzer Prize in the category Breaking News Photography.

John B. Moore is the senior photographer covering the Middle East and South Asia for Getty Images. He was also on the AP staff that won the 2005 Pulitzer Prize.

Muhammed Muheisen was on the AP staff that won the 2005 Pulitzer Prize in Breaking News Photography.

Staff Sgt. D. Myles-Cullen is a photographer for the US Air Force.

Tony Nicoletti, a photojournalist for the *British Daily Record*, was named the Scottish News Photographer of the Year in 2004.

Anja Niedringhaus is a German AP photographer who has covered every major conflict from the Balkans in the 1990s to the war in Iraq; she was the only woman on the team of eleven AP photographers awarded the 2005 Pulitzer Prize for Breaking News photography for their work in Iraq. In November of 2005 she was honored with the International Women's Media Foundation's Courage in Journalism Award.

Andrew Parsons works for the Press Association and the AP.

Laura Rauch is an AP photographer based in Las Vegas. Her work covering the wars in Afghanistan and Iraq was recognized by the AP Managing Editors with awards in 2002 and 2003.

Laurent Rebours is a chief photo editor and photographer for the AP.

Terry Richards was named Photographer of the Year at the 2004 British Press Awards.

Ivan Sekretarev was born in Moscow, worked extensively for the Russian press, then joined the Moscow branch of the AP in 1998. He has worked extensively in Chechnya and covered the wars in Afghanistan and Iraq, the 2004 Olympics, and elections in many former Soviet republics. He accompanied Presidents Yeltsin and Putin on many of their trips around the world.

Mohammed Uraibi was part of the AP team that won the 2005 Pulitzer Prize in the category Breaking News Photography.

John Moore

Stefan Zaklin is a freelance photographer from the US who works for the European Pressphoto Agency, Reuters, and the AP. Zaklin was a finalist in the 2002 Alexia Competition, which supports photography promoting world peace and cultural understanding.

Alexander Zemlianichenko is the chief photographer of the AP Moscow bureau. He won the 1997 Pulitzer Prize for his photo of Russian President Boris Yeltsin dancing at a rock concert prior to his election.

Sources:

www.ap.org | www.worldpressphoto.nl
www.DesMoinesRegister.com
www.editorandpublisher.com
www.poyi.org | www.iwmf.org | www.guardian.co.uk
www.dirckhalstead.org | www.jonmills.co.uk
www.knight.stanford.edu | www.ifex.org
www.lightstalkers.org | www.alexiafoundation.org
www.holdthefrontpage.co.uk | www.pulitzer.org
www.newsline.com.pk/NewsOct2002/photooct.htm